Walks on the

Helvellyn and Fairfield

by
Tom Bowker

Dalesman Books
1990

Key to Maps

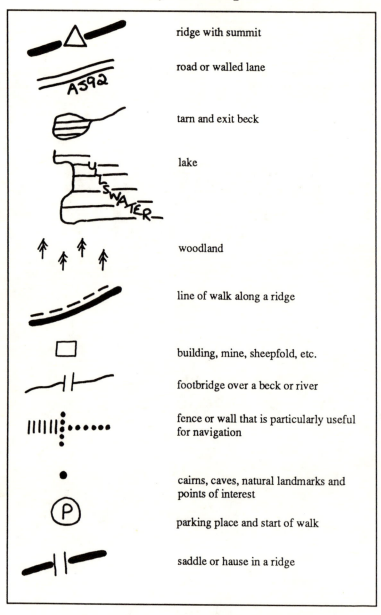

Contents

INTRODUCTION 4

FAIRFIELD
Walk 1	Fairfield and Seat Sandal via Allcock Tarn	6
Walk 2	Fairfield via Dovedale and The Priest's Hole	9
Walk 3	Fairfield via Deepdale and The Step	12
Walk 4	The Kirkstone Fells	14

GRISEDALE
Walk 5	Dollywaggon Pike to Sticks Pass via The Tongue	17
Walk 6	A Grisedale Round	20

HELVELLYN
Walk 7	The Helvellyn Classic	23
Walk 8	A Greenside Round	26
Walk 9	Place Fell and the Ullswater Shore Path	29
Walk 10	Helvellyn via Dunmail Raise	32
Walk 11	Exploring Helvellyn's Western Gills	35

THE DODS
Walk 12	Aira Force, Hartside and Great Dod	38
Walk 13	Around St. John's in the Vale via High Rigg and Fisher's Wife's Rake	41

MARATHON
Walk 14	Shap to Wasdale Head	45

THE DALESMAN PUBLISHING COMPANY LTD.,
CLAPHAM, via Lancaster, LA2 8EB

First published 1990

© TOM BOWKER 1990

ISBN: 0 85206 998 7

INTRODUCTION

THIS third book in a series offers walks on the Fairfield group of fells; the fells enclosing Grisedale; both flanks of the Helvellyn massif; and its northern outliers the Dods. As a guidebook writer I feel myself torn between an eagerness to introduce my readers to my beloved Lakeland fells, a natural desire that my books will sell, and a concern that I must accept some blame for the consequent erosion of mountain paths. With the latter in mind, I try to diverge from the 'motorways', e.g. the Fairfield Horeshoe, thus hoping to spread the load a little.

The walks described should be treated with due respect. Boots should be worn and rucksacks should contain waterproofs, spare clothing, map, compass, whistle and survival bag. In winter a torch, balaclava, mittens and some extra food should be added. When snow and ice coat the fells, an ice-axe should be carried. Crampons are becoming more commonly used by fellwalkers, and rightly so. Frequent practice in the use of map and compass make that winter day when their use suddenly becomes vital much less terrifying. Remember the cardinal rule — start using your compass from a point where you know where you are, don't wait until you are lost. Successful navigation through deteriorating conditions adds a bonus to your day and a boost to your confidence. Remember, in an emergency, all becks flow downhill and if followed with care can be fast escape routes in bad weather. Never be afraid to turn back. The fells will still be there next weekend.

Alongside each walk is a sketch map to be used in conjunction with the text. It is advisable, however, also to carry the relevant sheet of the 1:25000 The English Lakes Outdoor Leisure Maps. All the place names in the text refer to the 1982 edition of these maps. I have, however, preferred to use the old style 'Dod' rather than the upstart 'Dodd'. The mileages and heights of ascent are approximate. 'Left' or 'right' refers to a physical object as if facing it. Parking details are as per the maps, local authorities and tradition up to press, but are always liable to change. Limited space means I have to choose between detailed route descriptions, incidental information and detailed descriptions of views. I tend to be niggardly with the latter, feeling it's useful for walkers to attempt to orientate the view to their map.

The only way to learn about the fells is to be out regularly in all conditions. There will be times when you are frightened and times when you are physically exhausted. Ironically, these are the days that live most vividly in the memory and when you learn most about the mountains. Don't forget that it's a game, it's fun, it's adventure. For the fellwalker, given reasonable fitness and equipment, using his/her commonsense, the dangers are more apparent than real. Statistically, you are probably in more danger in your home or on your journey to and from the fells.

The Lakeland fells have become inextricably woven into the weft of my life.

My addiction to climbing them led to love, marriage and fatherhood, and innumerable friendships. They stimulated my interest in writing and are the bedrock of its continuing development. They have given me untold days of rewarding physical endeavour, good company, and wonderment at the beauty seen. If this booklet should bring such pleasures to any who read it I will be content. Happy walking!

Tom Bowker

FAIRFIELD

Walk 1

9 miles
3,200 feet of ascent

Fairfield and Seat Sandal via Allcock Tarn

A relatively easy but enjoyable outing, taking a more entertaining way up on to Heron Pike than the eroded 'flog' from Rydal. Seat Sandal is a bonus, though not compulsory, an isolated peak that cannot easily be fitted into the Helvellyn or Fairfield groups but worth the extra effort for the views.

Parking /Start: In the disused quarry below White Moss Common on the northern verge of the A591 just west of Rydal Water (GR:348066).

Leave the car park and walk a short way along the A591 verge, towards Rydal, to where a path climbs left through the trees. It emerges on to the end of a tarmac road near a tiny vegetated tarn. Wordsworth is reported to have skated here. I have disturbed a heron from its surface and deer in the trees further down the road. Walk left down the road to where a path signposted 'Allcock Tarn' forks right near a seat. Follow this path to and through a gate. Beyond, it winds pleasantly upwards through trees and around rocky outcrops, passing a delightful fishpond set in a stand of larch. As you climb the view of the Vale of Grasmere and its encircling fells expands munificently. At a fork ignore a path branching right to a metal gate and bear left across the fellside. Beyond a gate the path steepens towards a stand of trees partially hiding the rocky cone of Grey Crag. Higher, it swings left across a beck then across the steep fellside below the peak. Below lies the field where the famous Grasmere Sports are held. Runners in the Grasmere Fell Race toil up the slope below you, circle Grey Crag's summit, and plunge headlong down again to the finish. Climb further and you will see the metal flag-holder set amongst the summit rocks. Continue on to pass through a gap in a wall to reach the shore of Allcock Tarn.

Cross the dam, the beck beyond, and climb through an iron-barred gap in a wall. A faint path starts up the steepish fellside but tends to fade away as height is gained. It is simply a matter of picking the easiest line, getting your head down, and sooner than you think the angle will ease and you'll find yourself on the crest stumbling amongst the ruts of the Fairfield Horseshoe 'motorway'. Turn left over the summits of Heron Pike, 2,007 feet, and Erne Crag, 2,037 feet. An 'erne' was a sea-eagle, though it's a long time since one ever sailed over Fairfield. In the dip beyond a hump, Rydal Fell, 2,014 feet, straddles the narrowing ridge before a steep stony climb leads on to the summit of Great Rigg, 2,513 feet. A further dip gives way to a long steady climb up on to the broad stony summit dome of Fairfield, 2,863 feet.

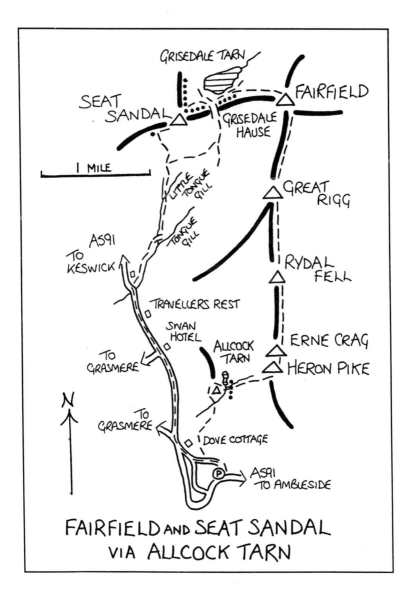

FAIRFIELD AND SEAT SANDAL VIA ALLCOCK TARN

Given the weather, wander round absorbing the views. Southwards gleam the waters of Windermere, Esthwaite, Coniston and far Morecambe Bay. Walk east and peer down into the rugged depths of Sleet Cove, with circumspection please if the rim is icy or corniced. Walk to the northern corner for another airy peep onto the rocky cone of Cofa Pike, with brawny St. Sunday Crag rising beyond. Northwards, Helvellyn displays the magnificent eastern coves and ridges that make it one of Britain's finest mountains. Westerly, the thrusting dome of Gable dominates a superb mountain skyline ranging from Coniston Old Man to Grisedale Pike.

One of the earliest recorded ascents of Fairfield was made by a party intent on bivouacing on the summit. Unlike the modern backpacker, they refused to sacrifice a modicum of comfort in order to save weight. They were accompanied by a horse and three guides, who between them carried thirty-six bottles of bitter beer, two bottles of gin, two bottles of sherry, one gallon of water, four loaves of bread, one leg of lamb, one leg of mutton, two fowl, one tongue, half a pound of cigars, four carriage lamps, two packs of playing cards and a large tent. During the night a storm blew down their tent, scattered their comestibles, and sent them, duly chastened and soaked, scurrying back down to Ambleside.

Head west from the central stone 'shelter' along a line of cairns leading on to a steep shaly path overlooking Grisedale Tarn, which eventually runs out alongside a wall on to the saddle of Grisedale Hause. (See Walk 10 regarding the ghostly legend of Grisedale Tarn.)

You can escape leftwards, through the gap in the wall, down Tongue Gill on to the A591. Otherwise, walk alongside the wall and climb a path slanting steeply right, then left, up the shaly flank of Seat Sandal. Presently the angle eases and the path follows the wall, passing a small tarn on its far side, on to the broad grassy summit. Go through a gap in the wall to the handsome summit cairn at 2,414 feet.

Head westerly towards a lower cairn, but before reaching it turn left (south) over the rim of the fell. Pick your way down the steep fellside, between scree fans and rock outcrops, eventually to join a crossing path. Follow this down grassy Little Tongue to the confluence of becks at the foot of the Great Tongue spur. Cross a footbridge into a walled lane leading down on to the A591. Turn left down the A591, bypassing Grasmere village, to the crossroads at Town End. Turn left and climb the road past Dove Cottage. Ignore the 'Rydal' road forking right and climb a little further to a junction with your outward route near the seat and 'Allcock Tarn' sign.

Walk 2

**8 miles
3100 feet of ascent**

Fairfield via Dovedale
and the Priest's Hole

Dovedale, with a popular pub and campsite at its foot and wide open to the gaze of passing visitors on the A592, is ripe for invasion. Nevertheless, it retains an air of isolation, especially when the pastoral lower reaches give way to a rugged dalehead dominated by Dove Crag. A scramble into its 'Priest's Hole' adds a dash of 'cloak and dagger' to your day. The rest is splendid high level fellwalking — who can ask for more?

Parking/Start: In the car park on the A592 near where it crosses the Goldrill Beck over Cow Bridge, at the entrance to the track alongside the west bank of Brotherswater :GR:403134).

    Go through the gate behind the car park and follow this track to pass Hartsop Hall Farm, and join a path from the Sykeside campsite. Turn right, shortly to pass to the right of farm buildings to reach a fork. Take the right fork, signposted 'Dove Crag'. Follow this below a derelict lead mine and through woodland to a gate leading out on to the open fellside. The valley ahead can be seen to narrow and swing leftwards, the path clinging to its right flank. Follow this pleasant path to where it curves and climbs left. Towering ahead now, above a sweep of scree and a tumble of massive weathered boulders, is Dove Crag. A climbing guide to the Eastern Fells modestly describes it as "one of the most impressive cliffs in England". Crick your neck at it and it's easy to understand why generations of Britain's finest climbers have trod this way to take up its stark challenge. Shortly after crossing a beck the path climbs steeply up to the right of the crag to reach a wet rocky corner, which can be avoided on the right. Beyond this corner the angle eases and from this point an interesting diversion leads into the 'Priest's Hole'.

    Turn left across a grass and scree slope to where an obvious rocky 'rake' leads left on to a ledge on the crag face. From here a path twists up on to a broad grassy ledge before the cave mouth, which is guarded by a low wall. Inside the cave there is a metal box containing a visitors' book. The latest editions of the Ordnance Survey two-and-a-half-inch maps appear to lend credence to the legend that this is no natural cave but a 'priest's hole' hacked or blasted out by sixteenth century fellsmen loyal to the Old Faith. As a born romantic I find this exciting. Physical facts substantiating the legend are that the cave is hidden from the valley floor and remains so until you virtually step into it. Little could move in the valley without being observed from the entrance ledge. Escape into the fastness of Fairfield is but a short climb away.

    Return to the path and climb into a boggy basin, passing to the left of a small shallow tarn. Beyond this steeper climbing and cairns lead on to the stony

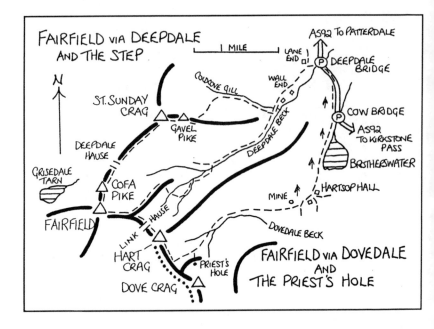

saddle dividing Dove Crag and Hart Crag, crowned by a wall, and a junction with the worn Fairfield Horseshoe path. Turn right and follow this path in a rocky climb to the cairn crowning the bouldery summit dome of Hart Crag, 2,698 feet.

Now descend north-west on to the grassy saddle of Link Hause, overlooking the rugged combe of Link Cove, dominated by the steep smooth rocks of Scrubby Crag. Beyond stretches drumlin-dimpled Deepdale. Climb north-west, then west, around and above Rydal Head, the dalehead of the valley encircled by the Fairfield Horseshoe. The path veers north-west, on to the Fairfield summit dome, across the head of a deeply cut scree chute curiously christened Flinty Grave. (Dickens would have snapped that name up.) A short walk along the rim of the flank falling precipitously into Sleet Cove reaches the scattering of cairns and rude wind shelters crowning the stony summit of Fairfield, 2,863 feet. (See Walk 1 for historical interest and a description of the views.)

From the northern corner of Fairfield summit head down a steep, shaly, worn path towards the rocky cone of Cofa Pike. Under snow treat this descent with great care, especially if you have no ice-axe, for a slip here could have nasty consequences. Under such conditions keep to the left flank of the ridge where the angle is less steep. From the dip below climb on to and across the pleasantly airy summit ridge of Cofa Pike, 2,500 feet. Beyond, a rocky ridge leads down on to the grassy saddle of Deepdale Hause. To your right, across Sleet Cove, the rocks of Hutaple Crag mount in tiers on to the knobbled skyline of The Step (see Walk 3). Leftwards, across Grisedale, are the delectably ice-carved and time-honed ridges and coves of Helvellyn.

From Deepdale Hause a grassy ridge, which continually surprises me by being steeper and longer than I expect it to be, leads to the cairn crowning the stony dome of St. Sunday Crag, 2,759 feet. Now head east towards the shapely cone of Gavel Pike. Descend the ridge beyond Gavel Pike into a dip below the hump of Lord's Seat. Slant left, then right, down into Cold Cove and bear left across its swampy slope to reach the bank of Coldcove Gill. Descend alongside this gill which becomes rockier, deeper, creamily-cascaded, and, given the time of year, flower with primrose, violet and wood sorrel. It eventually spills under a clapper bridge at the entrance to Deepdale.

Turn left across the bridge and follow the path past the dwelling at Wall End, and Deepdale Hall Farm, to a gate near the cottages at Lane End. Beyond the gate turn right down a walled track on to the A592 at Deepdale Bridge. Turn right along the verge to where a rocky outcrop blocks it. Climb up this and over a stile on to a path leading through woodland and above the road back to the car park.

Walk 3 7 miles
3,000 feet of ascent

Fairfield via Deepdale and The Step

The popular Lakeland fells are crowded with walkers. The shelves of Lakeland's bookshops are packed with fellwalking guidebooks. Words enough have been penned praising the Fairfield fells alone to fill Link Cove ankle deep in paper. Despite this, Deepdale, Link and Sleet Coves still retain an air of 'wilderness', especially in winter. A magnificent walk-cum-scramble and undoubtedly my favourite approach to Fairfield.

Parking/Start: On the verges of the A592 near the telephone box at Deepdale Bridge. GR:399144).

Cross the bridge and turn left at the 'Public Footpath' sign, with the legend 'Deepdale' also on the bridge wall to your left. Follow the rough walled track up to Lane End Cottages and turn left through a gate. Follow a path across a field to a right fork and a gate signposted 'Deepdale/Fairfield'. Follow a rough track, passing above 'Wall End', to enter Deepdale proper over a clapper bridge spanning Coldcove Gill. Habitation and ordered fields are left behind now as the path gradually curves right to reveal one of the wildest and most dramatic daleheads in Lakeland. From Grasmere, Fairfield looks big, but bovine and grassy. From Deepdale, Fairfield is every inch a mountain. From its excitingly cleft skyline crags, gullies and scree fans tumble into the shadowy bowls of high, ice-sculpted coves.

The walk up Deepdale is easy and as you go you can pick out the line of your proposed route. The rocky gully-split cone dominating the centre of the dalehead is Greenhow End. It terminates The Step, a crag-lined spur thrusting north-east from the Fairfield summit dome, dividing Link Cove from Sleet Cove. Your initial objective is Link Cove, the hanging valley to the left of Greenhow End as you approach. Scrutinise the fellside spilling out of Link Cove into Deepdale and you will see it is split by two gills linked by a band of crags. Your target is the waterfall at the foot of the left-hand, more deeply cleft, Link Cove Gill.

When the drumlins that dimple the head of Deepdale are reached the main path climbs right, towards Sleet Cove. You head leftwards alongside the beck issuing from your target gill. Way beck in the mists of time I camped amidst these drumlins in a cotton tent that was minus such luxuries as a fly-sheet and sewn-in groundsheet. We were there, as I recall, on a weekend meet of the Gritstone Club, of which my pal Derek was keen to become a member. My most vivid memory is of a roaring wood fire around which we sat talking mountains until the early hours, whilst beyond the circle of our flamelit faces the fells staked out their dark promontories upon a sea of stars.

Having reached the waterfall at the foot of your gill, climb alongside it and pleasantly up the watercourse above to a pool at the foot of a waterfall where the ravine narrows. Climbed directly from hereon the gill is a serious 'scramble' requiring nerve, agility and a rope for protection here and there. Lesser mortals, like yours truly, now scramble up the rocks bounding the right bank of the gill. When dry these give easy and enjoyable scrambling with airy views down on to the cascades. When the gill begins to lean back extend your scrambling up its slabby bed. Where the gill turns more sharply left, and before reaching a beck cascading over its right bank, climb right to cross a broad grassy ridge. Descend into the hollow beyond, crossing a beck, and climb up to the base of the rocks flanking Greenhow End. As you approach look for a grassy rake slanting right through these rocks. The rake is cairned and the rightward slant leads to a shallow gully slanting leftward, followed by a grassy terrace slanting right onto the crest of The Step. (An enjoyable 'scrambly' alternative, given dry conditions, is to start by a tree a few yards left of the foot of the rake and pick the most interesting line up the clean slabby rocks above, crossing the shallow gully and upper terrace of the 'rake' before emerging on to the crest of The Step.)

Now follow the well-defined and pleasantly rocky ridge with the rocks of Hutaple Crag falling precipitously away to your right. Eventually the ridge broadens, and from the head of a wide stone gully there is a vertiginous view of crag, gully, and scree fan plunging from the north-eastern rim of Fairfield into the stony depths of Sleet Cove. Beyond Sleet Cove's far rim, topped by the rocky cone of Cofa Pike, the Helvellyn outliers rank shoulder to brawny shoulder with their chief. Follow the broadening ridge to its junction with the Fairfield summit dome near the head of a scree gully. Continue ahead to join the eroded 'Horseshoe' path climbing right towards the top, or, more pleasantly, cross the head of the scree gully, follow the rim of Sleet Cove to rejoin the 'Horseshoe' path near the head of the scree chute christened Flinty Grave and follow it on to the summit of Fairfield, 2,863 feet. (See Walk 1 from 'Given the weather . . . for a description of the view and historical notes.)

Now follow the description in Walk 2, from 'From the northern corner of Fairfield summit . . .', for the return leg of your walk over Cofa Pike and St. Sunday Crag.

Walk 4

**8 miles
3,400 feet of ascent**

The Kirkstone Fells

A fine walk that 'rounds up' three interesting fells which tend to be isolated from their main groups. A walk that offers much of interest — old quarries, possible deer sightings, varied views and a surprising amount of easy rock scrambling. From most angles these fells could be dismissed as 'puddens', but from near Hartsop Hall Farm you become aware that these are three very graceful and steeply sculpted hills.
Parking/Start: On the north side of Caudale Bridge where the A592 crosses the Caudale Beck, about a quarter of a mile south of the Brotherswater Hotel. GR:402115).

Go through the metal gate on the south side of the bridge and climb the path alongside the beck. Soon it turns away from the beck and spirals up a steep grassy ridge. As you climb there is a fine view backwards into Dovedale, dominated by the pale steep rocks of Dove Crag. Rising above the Hartsop-above-Row ridge are the knobbly skylines of Fairfield and St. Sunday Crag. The spirals you are climbing are the remains of an old 'sledgate' down which quarrymen steered sleds, or 'trailbarrows', loaded with a quarter of a ton of slate, running before their creaking loads like a horse. The old quarry overlooks Caudale, a lonely mountain sanctuary which is often the haunt of red deer, and if you delight in exploring such sites follow the path forking left from the ridge crest. At the end of your exploration climb the slope above the quarry to regain the ridge path. Incidentally, I've also spotted deer picking their way across the shaly west flank of the ridge, seemingly oblivious to the summer traffic jamming the Kirkstone zig-zags below them.

For some reason known only to the cartographer the upper part of the ridge is emblazoned 'Rough Edge' on the later $2^1/_2$ inch maps, although it's largely grassy. As this 'edge' flattens out into the summit dome the path becomes indistinct, but if the Caudale rim is followed a large cairn soon looms ahead. From this cairn head south-easterly across the broad grassland, passing an unnamed tarn, to join a path alongside a wall. Turn left along this to a gap in a crossing wall. Go through the gap and walk a few yards north-easterly to reach the summit cairn of Stony Cove Pike, 2,503 feet.

To descend, go back through the gap and walk back alongside the wall heading westerly. Where it turns south-westerly there is, a short walk away to your right and overlooking Kirkstone Pass, a memorial to one Mark Atkinson, a licensee of the Kirkstone Pass Inn for many years. Follow the wall south-westerly into a dip, then over the rocky hump of St. Raven's Edge, before descending westerly to emerge on to the A592 near the Kirkstone Pass Inn.

From the car park across the road attack the craggy south-eastern flank of Red Screes. The route is obvious, a fault line running diagonally from left to right through the crags. Easier alternatives can be found by bearing left into

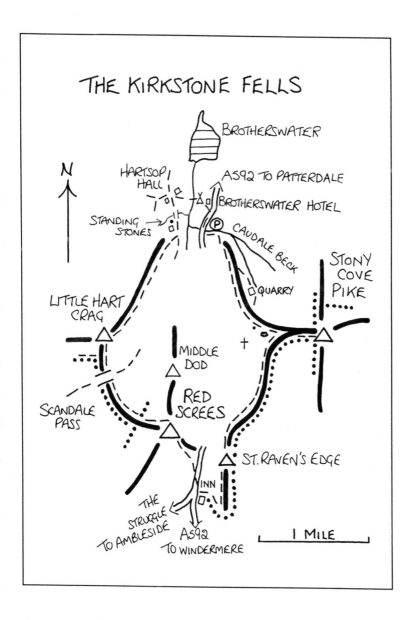

the combe whose sanguine crags and screes give the mountain its name. The tumbled wall straggling up the grassy slopes below the combe was listed in the Troutbeck Painable Fence Book of 1680. Walls had to be maintained on 'pain' of a fine of 8s.6d! The fault line is an easy but exhilarating ascent, especially under snow, with a fine sense of space around and below. You might find yourself looking down into the cockpit of a jet fighter as it screams through the pass! The rocks give way to easier-angled grass leading on to the summit of Red Screes, 2,545 feet. Cairn and trig-point stand on the precipitous northern rim overlooking the spirals of the A592 and Brotherswater. The summit is broad and grassy, and a shallow tarn nestles close to the trig-point. The view in the south-to-northwest arc, from gleaming Windermere's flotilla of dark wooded isles to Helvellyn's high and hoary dome, is superb.

Descend west down gentle grass slopes to a junction of walls. Follow the wall heading north-westerly down steepening slopes on to the saddle of Scandale Pass. Climb up the far slope alongside the wall until it turns left. Leave the wall corner and climb north towards the left-hand summit of surprisingly craggy Little Hart Crag, 2,091 feet. The summit rocks offer a short but entertaining scramble to attain the cairn. Dove Crag can now be seen in profile, a true guide to its unrelenting steepness.

Descend north-easterly over the subsidiary top and along a broad ridge which narrows and steepens down into Dovedale. At its base, near a barn, join the path that links Patterdale and Ambleside via Scandale Pass. Turn left and follow it through 'standing stones', across a footbridge and through sheep pens close to farm buildings, to emerge on to the Dove Crag path above Hartsop Hall Farm. Turn right towards the farm, then right again on to a path leading across fields and into the Sykeside Campsite below the Brotherswater Hotel. A pint at the hotel will set you up nicely for the short walk back up the road to your car.

GRISEDALE

Walk 5

12 miles
3,500 feet of ascent

Dollywaggon Pike to Sticks Pass via The Tongue

Striding and Swirrel are justifiably Helvellyn's most popular 'edges'. Dollywaggon Pike and Nethermost Pike, however, each thrust a fine ridge into the eastern coves. Both have narrow rocky sections, though neither is as narrow or sustained for as long as on their more glamorous neighbours. A rewarding feature of these ridges, however, is that you don't have to queue. The walk described below climbs Dollywaggon Pike by the Tongue before marching north to Sticks Pass over all the knobbles of Helvellyn's mountain backbone. A rewarding 'bag' of seven peaks over two thousand feet.

Parking/Start: Patterdale. A metered car park has been recently opened almost opposite the Patterdale Hotel. There's also limited parking space at the foot of the lane leading into Grisedale.

Climb this twisting tarmac lane into Grisedale to a gate with a slate sign 'Grasmere/Grisedale Tarn' on the wall to its left and 'Footpath to Helvellyn' on the wall to its right. Go through the gate and head up the valley. St. Sunday Crag now peers over the fellside to your left. Ahead, two prominent ridges thrust out above Grisedale. The humped left-hand ridge is The Tongue, your objective. The pointed right-hand ridge is Nethermost Edge. Ruthwaite Cove hangs between them, and Nethermost Cove between Nethermost Edge and Striding Edge, the bulky ridge to its right.

Ignore a farm road turning right and continue ahead, shortly to pass the dwelling at Elmhow. Readers who watched the enjoyable television drama serial 'Fell Tiger' some years ago may recognise in this building the home of the hero. Go through a gate to the left of a barn and on past a plantation. Ignore a path forking right to a footbridge over Grisedale Beck. Climb on past a rocky hump to cross the beck at a higher point by a second footbridge. Climb the path on the far bank to a junction with a crossing path close to Ruthwaite Lodge, now the climbing hut of the Sheffield University M.C. I first sought shelter in Ruthwaite Lodge on a bleak winter day in 1952. It was then a windswept shell ankle deep in sheep dung. Above and to the right of the hut, Ruthwaite Beck cascades over slabby rocks near the remains of old mine workings. Climb to the right of the hut up a faint path through the bracken. Higher, the path curves right below a rocky hump to reach and cross a beck. Do not follow it across the beck but climb the grassy slopes on the left of the beck towards the foot of an obvious grassy, and narrowing, gully breaching the rocky flank of The Tongue. Climb this steepish but easy gully eventually to emerge on to

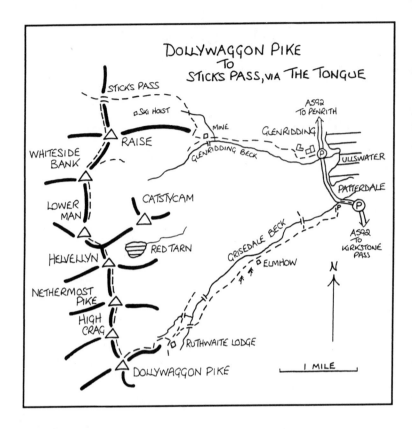

the grassy crest of The Tongue. On our last ascent of this gully we found it resplendent with mountain flowers — Wild Thyme, Heath Bedstraw, Tormentil, the delicate and delectable Eyebright, Moss Saxifrage and Yellow Mountain Saxifrage.

Now follow the ridge crest, seeking 'scrambly bits' wherever you can, eventually to emerge slap-bang up against the cairn crowning Dollywaggon Pike, 2,814 feet. As you climb look right, across the depths of Ruthwaite Cove, and spot tiny Hard Tarn tucked in its slabby pocket below the south flank of Nethermost Edge. From the Dollywaggon cairn follow a path curving northwards along the fell rim, over a hump and down on to the saddle at the head of Ruthwaite Cove to join the eroded 'tourist' path. This path leads eventually to the summit of Helvellyn but on the way inexplicably skirts all the intervening summits, thus missing a 'bag' of two fine peaks and the splendid 'bird's-eye' views into rugged coves and down a chequered dale to the shimmering twists of Ullswater. Don't be lured by its insidious, slothful appeal for your purpose is 'to strive, to seek, to find', to sweat a bit, 'bag' peaks, and be rewarded by superb Lakeland panoramas and the gratification physical effort brings.

Climb out of the saddle above Ruthwaite Cove, initially along the 'tourist' path, to where a path forks steeply right. Climb this to reach the cairn crowning the grassy summit of High Crag, 2,896 feet. Head north along the fell rim into a dip then up on to the wide turfy dome of Nethermost Pike, 2,923 feet. Across it a line of cairns march northwards, passing to the left of the summit cairn which stands close to the dome's northern rim, overlooking Nethermost Cove. In the dip beyond Nethermost Pike rejoin the 'tourist' route which begins its climb towards Helvellyn top. Given clear weather, ignore it and follow the fell rim to reach the memorial cairn (see Walk 7) crowning the shaly exit slope above Striding Edge. This view of the famous ridge has graced a zillion calendars and postcards and, though now showing signs of wear and tear, still has the power to thrill, especially when cloaked in sunlight and snow. 'That prodigious Precipice of grey stone with deep Wrinkles facing me' was Coleridge's awed description of a moonlit Striding Edge. Throughout this description I have been advocating following the fell rim rather than the eroded paths set back from it. In winter or 'white-out' conditions, however, follow this practice with care, for unstable cornices build up along the rim and winter winds scour snow into ice.

Continue along the rim to reach the wind shelter tucked under the summit rocks and take a well-earned 'breather', if you can find elbow room. Climb above the shelter on to the summit rocks of Helvellyn, 3,116 feet. The trig-point to the north-west is a metre lower according to the map. If you visit both you can't go wrong. Should the mountain gods in their mercy grant you the boon of a clear day then every drop of sweat, every creaking muscle, will have been a miserly sacrifice in return for the sublimity of mountains heaped around you.

Head north-westerly along the fell rim, passing the trig-point, When the cairn marking the start of the descent on to Swirrel Edge is passed the rim veers more westerly and leads you down into a dip below the summit of Lower Man, 3,033 feet. (A path leads from the trig-point into this dip should the rim route be hazardous.) Climb north on to this summit before descending a stony ridge on to the saddle below Whiteside Bank. To your right, across the depths of Brown Cove, looms Catstycam, in form one of the fairest of Lakeland's fells. Now a short climb just west of north brings you to the cairn crowning Whiteside Bank, 2,832 feet. A north-easterly descent leads on to a grassy saddle where a path forks right and down into Keppel Cove. It provides a possible 'escape' route, but I'm sure you will have enough energy left to ignore it and climb on to 'bag' Raise, 2,896 feet, your final peak of the day.

It's downhill all the way now. A path heads north on to the grassy saddle of Sticks Pass where a smart right-turn takes you down and alongside Sticks Gill into the hanging valley cupping the boggy bed of a disused mines reservoir and extensive spoil heaps. You will find samples of galena if you care to fossick among them. After passing through the spoil heaps the path drops over the rim of the corrie, zig-zagging down over more spoil heaps and through dwarf juniper to reach the old mine buildings of the Greenside Lead Mine (see Walk 7). Pass through the buildings and follow the rough road past the Greenside Youth Hostel down into Glenridding. Just under a mile along the A592 leads you back to Patterdale.

Obviously this walk could be as easily done from Glenridding, either by walking along the A592 to the lane leading into Grisedale, or by climbing the path past Lanty's Tarn, descending into Grisedale and following the path above the north-west bank of Grisedale Beck to Ruthwaite Lodge.

Walk 6   11 miles
4,500 feet of ascent

A Grisedale Round

The summit of Nethermost Pike is a broad turfy dome. From Grisedale, however, the fell deceives us into believing it is a dramatic cone approached by a wickedly steep and narrow-looking ridge. If we allow ourselves to go along with this deceit we will be rewarded by an exploration of a high, lonely combe, some interesting old mine workings, and an unfortunately short but nevertheless pleasantly narrow and rocky arete. By the time we tread the Nethermost dome we will have forgiven it its attempt to deceive. To continue over the fells encircling Grisedale makes for a rewarding mountain day.

Parking/Start: As for Walk 5.

Follow the description given in Walk 5 as far as the gate with the 'Footpath to Helvellyn' sign on its right. Turn right here and follow this signpost down and across the Grisedale Beck and up the far fellside to a gate in a wall corner. Go through the gate and turn left to follow the path heading up the valley alongside a wall. Follow this path for well over a mile, with Nethermost Pike towering ahead and looking more impressive with every onward step. Just after passing above the Broomhill Plantation, and before reaching the footbridge over the Nethermostcove Beck, look for a narrow path forking

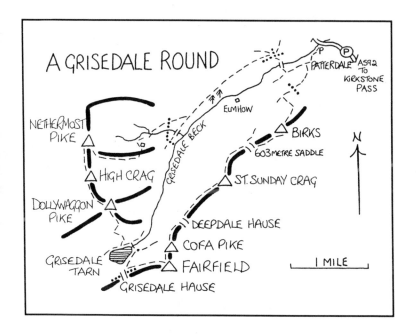

right through the bracken. There is a prominent upright boulder hereabouts. (If you miss the path and find yourself at the footbridge over the beck turn right and follow the right bank of the beck). Path, or beck bank, will both bring you to a wall spanned by a stone stile. Cross the stile and climb what appears to be a miners' path, fairly overgrown up the right bank of Nethermostcove Beck. The path ultimately fords the beck just below a delightful waterfall. After some searching its continuation should be found zig-zagging up the far bank.

Above the crags to your left stand the old mine workings that are your next objective. The angle eases as the path curves leftwards with the beck into the mouth of Nethermost Cove. (Nethermost Cove tends to be left to the solitary, the queues forming along the high stony rim of its northern fence — Striding Edge. It is a high mountain sanctuary whose peace is broken only by querulous sheep, the flutter of wind in the high crags and the clear unending cadences of cascading water, the signature tune of Lakeland. For the properly equipped fellwalker who likes to try the occasional straightforward snow climb, the headwall of the cove offers exciting possibilities. In good conditions a broad snow ramp slants from left to right up the headwall, giving several hundred feet of entertaining climbing, and is often crowned with an impressive cornice. This is venturing into the realm of 'mountaineering', however, and on the occasions we've climbed this route we've carried a rope and 'tied-on' for the exit over the cornice).

The path becomes indistinct in the entrance to the cove. Look for a prominent boulder which I recently took the liberty to crown with a small cairn. Climb left from the boulder towards the rim of the crags previously mentioned. With luck you should find some old mine workings, including one deep narrow shaft just beyond the shell of a workshop. Please don't fall into it! We've found specimens of galena in the surrounding spoil. Just beyond is a flooded shaft. Climb right above this to reach a cairn. From the cairn a largely grassy ridge undulates up to the base of the impressive rocky cone supporting Nethermost Edge. Follow the ridge, adhering to its rockier right-hand rim for the views down into Nethermost Cove. The final climb up on to Nethermost Edge is steep and rocky but presents little difficulty, a path taking the easiest line. The scramble along the Edge is unfortunately a brief one but exhilarating for all that. The rocks give way to a steeper grassy exit slope debouching on to the summit dome. Walk a short way north-westerly to reach the cairn crowning Nethermost Pike, 2,923 feet.

Now follow a line of cairns south across the summit dome into a dip. Climb leftwards out of the dip, along the fell rim, to reach the cairn crowning High Crag, 2,896 feet. Now follow the fell rim south down on to the saddle at the head of Ruthwaite Cove and a junction with the eroded main ridge 'tourist' path. Climb along this out of the saddle, but shortly fork left on a fainter path following the fell rim. Follow this over a hump then on to a steeper climb leftwards to reach the cairn crowning the summit of Dollywaggon Pike, 2,814 feet. Descend south, following the fell rim around the head of Cock Cove to rejoin the 'tourist' path, which wimpishly skirts the summit of Dollywaggon Pike, leading onto the steep zig-zags bringing you down on to the shore of Grisedale Tarn. Turn left. Should lack of fitness or deteriorating weather suggest a return valleywards at this point, simply follow this path down into the head of Grisedale ultimately to rejoin your outward route. If, however, the weather's all right and you're still 'raring to go', when you reach the end of the tarn turn right and cross Grisedale Beck where it exits from the tarn. Now climb the path slanting right, above the tarn, into the gap in the old wall crowning the saddle of Grisedale Hause. Don't go through the gap but turn left alongside the wall and begin the steep nine hundred foot climb which ultimately leads you on to the summit dome of Fairfield, 2,863 feet. (See Walk 1 for scenic and historical notes regarding this summit). For the next section of your round, the traverse of Cofa Pike and the ascent of St. Sunday Crag, see the description in Walk 2 from "From the northern corner of Fairfield summit" to "the stony dome of St. Sunday Crag, 2,579 feet".

From the summit cairn of St. Sunday Crag you now head north, then north-easterly, down a largely grassy ridge on to the 603 metre saddle below Birks. Here, a path forks left to bypass this summit. I see little merit in following this, unless the weather is execrable, but much in climbing easily north-easterly to the diminutive cairn crowning the relatively unfrequented summit of Birks, 2,040 feet. Beyond the cairn the faint path swings left and down to rejoin the 'flunking' path on a grassy shelf. Turn right and follow this down to a stile over a wall. This descending path gives a fine view over the head of Ullswater. After passing through trees a stile is crossed and a turn left made down to a gate leading on to the lane at the entrance at Grisedale and a junction with your outward route.

HELVELLYN

Walk 7

9 miles
3,000 feet of ascent

The Helvellyn Classic

One of the most popular of British fell walks. Because of its popularity it's become a little battered and shopworn, but nevertheless still has the power to excite and thrill. When plastered in snow or ice it steps out of the league of 'mild scrambling' and becomes a serious proposition, warranting the use of ice-axe, crampons and possibly a rope.

Parking/Start: National ~~Trust~~ Park car park in Glenridding. (GR:386169).

Go back to the main road, turn right over the bridge and right again up the lane past the climbing shop. Continue until the path forks. Take the right-hand fork, signposted 'Greenside', to go between the beck and the campsite to reach and cross a stone bridge. Beyond this turn left up a rough track alongside a wall to a gate/stile signposted 'Helvellyn via Mires Beck'. Cross this and climb left to a similar sign on a wall directing you right up to a gate/stile in a wall corner. Beyond this turn left across a footbridge over a beck. Now climb the path up the right bank of Mires Beck, shortly crossing over to the left bank. A long steepish climb follows, the path eventually climbing alongside a wall, before the grassy summit of Birkhouse Moor, 2,355 feet, is attained. The view back of the constant changes of light on the shining reaches of Ullswater is a good excuse for 'breathers'. Some 'peak-baggers' lists credit Birkhouse Moor with three summits, but I feel that's a trifle generous. My list makes the highest point just to the right of the wall corner where the wall veers south-westerly towards Striding Edge. The 2-and-a-half-inch map argues the next bump that way — take your pick.

Hopefully, displayed before you now are the famous 'edges' enfolding the high corrie cupping Red Tarn and airily linking Helvellyn's 'table mountain' with conical Catstycam. Perhaps I should liken Helvellyn more to a giant aircraft carrier. In 1926 two daring young men landed their flying machine upon its summit and then, more daringly, took off from it. A memorial to this feat stands just south of the summit shelter. Continue, a little swampily, alongside the wall until it turns away at the Hole-in-the-Wall and you start the climb towards Striding Edge. Leave the worn path and climb the obvious summit overlooking the start of the 'edge' proper. This is High Spying How, 2,832 feet, and listed as a separate peak.

Once on Striding Edge the way is obvious. Don't be deterred by the metal cross just below and to the left after the first narrow section, a memorial to an unfortunate follower of foxhounds, the danger is more apparent than real. Unless you find it too scary, or ice or snow conditions forcibly prevent it, attempt to keep to the crest all the way. This gives the excitement, fun and

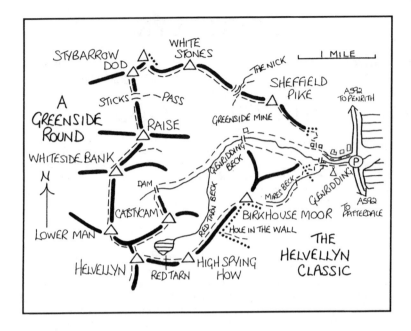

satisfaction that is the point of an ascent by this route. The most difficult section is the climb down into the gap at the end of the Edge, but even here the holds are large and firm. Beyond this gap there is another hump of rock to scramble over and then the route degenerates into a steep, shaly pant up on to the fell rim, emerging near a memorial to a doggy who maintained a long and loyal vigil over the corpse of his master, earning poetic praise from Wordsworth and Sir Walter Scott. There is a school of thought, admittedly largely composed of cat lovers, who believe Faithful Fido fortified himself with bits of Master.

Walk right along the rim of the fell shortly to reach the invariably crowded wind-shelter just below the summit rocks of Helvellyn, 3,116 feet. The view from Helvellyn is panoramic and I have not the space to describe it. It is a good place, on a clear windless day, to take out your map and orientate yourself to the splendours of Lakeland spread at your feet. The first recorded ascent of Helvellyn was made in 1791 by a Captain Joseph Budworth, a one-armed veteran of the Siege of Gibraltar, who celebrated his ascent by gleefully trundling boulders off the summit. Not a pursuit advocated in the Country Code, especially on weekends or Bank Holidays!

Walk north-westerly along the rim, passing the slightly lower trig-point, to a cairn on the rim, where it wears west-north-westerly, marking the start of the descent on to Swirrel Edge. After heavy snowfalls large cornices build up along this rim. In 'white-out' conditions they can, and have been, death traps for the unwary. Swirrel Edge is much easier and shorter than its big brother across Red Tarn, only a couple of rocky steps requiring care. At its lowest point a path forks right, down towards Red Tarn. Ignore this and climb along the ridge, broad and easy now, on to the narrow summit of Catstycam, 2,919 feet, a graceful, relatively unfrequented peak, splendid viewpoint and worth every gasp of extra effort.

Turn left and descend a steepish stony path down the fell's north-west ridge to a 'busted' dam spanning Glenridding Beck. In the 1920s water was stored in Keppel Cove, to your left, to power the Greenside Lead Mine smelters. The dam burst, loosing millions of gallons of water which, clawing up boulders and trees en route, poured into Glenridding village causing extensive damage but fortunately no loss of life. Cross the crest of the dam. If it's at all gusty you will probably regard this crossing as more scary than anything on the famous 'edges'. I know I have.

Follow the track on the far side down to the buildings of the old Greenside Lead Mine, now an outdoor pursuits centre. The mine was in production from 1780 to 1962, producing over one quarter of a million tons of lead concentrate. Just above the buildings cross back over Glenridding Beck by a footbridge and turn left along a pleasant path traversing below the steep and craggy Blea Cove flank of Birkhouse Moor to rejoin your outward route at a gate/stile.

Walk 8   **10 miles**
                                                                           4,000 feet of ascent

A Greenside Round

A walk of infinite variety, ranging from the broad grassland Dod country to the airy cragginess of Swirrel Edge and Catstycam. The start will make you puff so don't have too heavy a breakfast. Sheffield Pike gives fine views of Ullswater and an unusual look at Helvellyn.

Parking/Start: As for Walk 7.

    Walk up on to the upper level of the car park and follow a 'Helvellyn/Red Tarn' sign through a gap between buildings on to Greenside Road. Turn left and walk up the street, passing the Travellers Rest, to a fork. Follow the tarmac, climbing steeply right and signposted 'Greenside Youth Hostel', to where the road surface deteriorates. Continue past a terrace of houses then, beyond a cattle grid, fork right up a grassy path leading towards the rear of another terrace of houses. Duck under the washing lines to follow a narrowing path slanting left up the heathery fellside. It eventually 'zags' back to the right, passing a metal 'Footpath' sign, to join a path slanting left just below the grassy saddle above Blaes Crag. Turn left and climb this path which eventually levels out on to a grassy saddle crowned by a wall. Above you, Sheffield Pike offers a shapely rocky challenge.

    Don't go through the gap in the wall but turn left, alongside it, on a path which climbs on to a rocky, heathery ridge before swinging right through a gap in a wall. Now follow its twisting course, at a fairly unrelenting angle, for around seven hundred feet before emerging abruptly onto a surprisingly broad and heathery summit dome. The late Lakeland writer Graham Sutton wrote, 'Views are like bootlaces, they are a good excuse for stopping on the way up.' You have every excuse for a 'breather' over this stretch for the views are splendid. Away to your right, with luck, the sun will be glinting off mile after glistening mile of Ullswater, whilst to your left the dark elegant cone of Catstycam, 'the cat's ladder', is superimposed upon the battleship grey of 'flat-top' Helvellyn. ('Flat-top' is American slang for aircraft-carrier. Well, H.M.S. Helvellyn looks like a 'flat-top' if you're not too fussy, and was used as one back in 1926, see Walk 7.) The path across the summit dome tends to get lost among the heathery hummocks and swampy pools, but a north-westerly heading will bring you to the handsome cairn crowning Sheffield Pike, 2,214 feet.

    Now descend just north of west on to the broad grassy saddle of Nick Head. Cross the head of a beck, The Nick, and a crossing path climbing out of Glencoyne, and climb north-westerly up a steepening grass ridge. Higher, the ridge squeezes between the rim of a large disused quarry and craggy slopes falling precipitously into Glencoyne. Eventually the angle eases and the cairn crowning White Stones, 2,608 feet, is reached. (On earlier maps this summit was often labelled 'Greenside'.) Descend west on to a broad grassy saddle followed by a steepish climb up onto the north-eastern and highest summit of Stybarrow Dod, 2,765 feet. As you puff over the crest a fabulous array of fells rise up to greet you, Blencathra and Skiddaw being particularly prominent to the north and north-west. A length of wall just north-east of the cairn provides a useful windbreak should you feel like a 'breather'.

Head south-west over the subsidiary top, then veer south down on to the grassy saddle of Sticks Pass. The pass derives its name from the stakes once placed at regular intervals to guide travellers over it in poor visibility. Ore from the Greenside Mine used to be packed over here for smelting in Keswick. Look left up the northern flank of Raise to spot the ski-tow of the Lake District Ski Club. If fatigue or bad weather is eroding the physique or morale of your party a smart left turn on Sticks Pass will lead you easily back down to Glenridding. Otherwise, climb south, over initially swampy ground which becomes stonier and steeper, to 'bag' the rocky summit of Raise, 2,889 feet. Raise summit appears to be suffering from an outbreak of geological eczema, being crowned by an eruption of repulsive scabby-looking rocks.

All the hard work is virtually over now and the just reward for all your endeavours — the brow of the mighty Helvellyn and the elegant cone of Catstycam — rise proudly ahead. Descend south-westerly on to a grassy saddle where a path slanting back to your left along the rim of the fell offers an 'escape' route down into Keppel Cove, if required. A short climb 'bags' the innocuous summit of Whiteside Bank, 2,832 feet. Innocuous or not, to the peak-bagger (Munro bless us) they all count. Another dip leads on to the stony ridge whose ascent brings you to the cairn crowning Helvellyn Lower Man, 3,033 feet. From the shallow dip beyond this summit a boot-beaten highway climbs gently south-easterly to reach the trig-point crowning Helvellyn's much trodden but still high and mighty dome. A few yards east of the trig-point the ground plunges precipitously. Below, enfolded in the stony arms of Striding Edge and Swirrel Edge, Red Tarn glints darkly. You may find it hard to believe but in 1951, when skis were somewhat primitive and 'apres-ski' gear probably the same hairy tweeds donned for fellwalking, the slope plunging beneath your twitching toecaps was skied. In winter be circumspect in your peeks over this fell rim. After heavy snowfalls large cornices build up along it, and icy winds can make the summit dome a skating rink. Walk past the trig-point to the rocky hummock that is the true summit of Helvellyn, 3,116 feet. A wind-shelter, invariably crowded, lies just beyond. Just south of the wind-shelter is the tablet commemorating the mad but magnificent young men who landed their flying machine on Helvellyn in 1926.

To descend, walk back from the summit along the fell rim, passing the trig-point, to where a cairn on the rim marks the start of the path leading on to Swirrel Edge. Winter conditions excepting, when parties should be properly equipped, Swirrel Edge gives straightforward easy rock scrambling. Stick to the crest to obtain the sense of adventure, the 'fun' of the crossing. At the lowest point of the Edge a path forks right down towards Red Tarn. Ignore this and climb along the ridge, broad and stony now, to reach the summit of Catstycam, 2,919 feet.

I doubt if I will ever make a truly carefree ascent of Catstycam again. On Mayday in 1988 I was leading a party on this walk when we were caught in a thunderstorm on Helvellyn. In the clear period that followed we scurried across Swirrel Edge and up on to Catstycam to find to our horror the narrow summit occupied by the body of a walker who had been struck by lightning. Whilst one of our party raced for help we strove in vain to revive the stricken man. Another fierce thunderstorm swept over us as we did so, a storm in which, we were later to learn, yet another walker had been killed by lightning on Fairfield's outlier, Great Rigg. It was a tragic and unforgettable experience that forcibly brought home to me that even upon Lakeland's lowly mountains one must remain vigilant against the forces of nature.

From Catstycam it's downhill all the way. Turn left and descend the fell's steep stony north-west ridge to the partially demolished dam spanning the Glenridding Beck below Brown and Keppel Coves. Cross the dam, with care if there's a strong or gusty wind blowing. Now follow the rough former miners' track down to the buildings of the former Greenside Lead Mine, now an outdoor pursuits centre. Pass between the buildings, and the lower Youth Hostel, and follow the track down the valley to a junction with your outward route.

Walk 9

**8 miles
2,200 feet of ascent**

Place Fell and the Ullswater Shore Path

Place Fell is really an outlier of the High Street range and separated from the Helvellyn/Fairfield group by the headwaters of Ullswater, the meadows of the Vale of Patterdale and the A592. This should ensure its exclusion from this guidebook, but as the most convenient starting point for this walk is Patterdale village I'm taking the liberty of including it. It is an entertaining walk that is nowhere strenuous, all the hard work being done in the first two miles. The view from the summit is panoramic. The shore path is delightful, possibly the best of its kind in Lakeland, offering ever-changing views of woodland, water and mountains, and the opportunity for an impromptu swim or lakeside picnic. I've frequently spotted deer on Place Fell.

Parking/Start: As for Walk 5.

Walk south through Patterdale village, passing the White Lion Hotel, to where a bridge on your left spans Goldrill Beck. Cross the bridge and follow the road into the hamlet of Rooking where it curves left to a gate leading on to the open fellside. Go through the gate, cross a footbridge over a beck and climb the path slanting steeply right up the fellside, ultimately to emerge on to the grassy saddle of Boardale Hause. Surprisingly, I've spotted deer on the fellside below this popular path. Look for a metal manhole cover in the rear left-hand corner of this flattish saddle. Follow a path past this which shortly turns left to pass a small sheepfold and begins to climb towards the steep summit slopes of Place Fell. Steeper zig-zags eventually take you on to the left-hand skyline where a shaly gully leads up to the cairn crowning the subsidiary summit of Round How and the end of all the 'hard graft'. Easy walking along the westerly rim of the fell leads to the rocky tor and trig-point crowning Place Fell, 2,155 feet.

This summit is an ideal vantage point for taking out your map and orientating yourself with the Helvellyn/Fairfield fells, given of course that you can see them or there's not a map-snatching wind gusting across the summit. Their rugged ice-honed eastern flanks are particularly detailed. Away to the north-west Blencathra displays its fluted Threlkeld flank, with a retiring flat-topped Skiddaw to its left. Northwards, through the gap between Carrock Fell and isolated Great Mell Fell, lie the Solway Firth and Scotland.

To descend, head north to a pointed and cairned feature christened The Knight. Beyond this the path veers north-easterly down a rocky groove, then more steeply down to the sheepfold crowning the saddle of Low Moss. A slightly more direct route leads north-east from the summit to the Low Moss

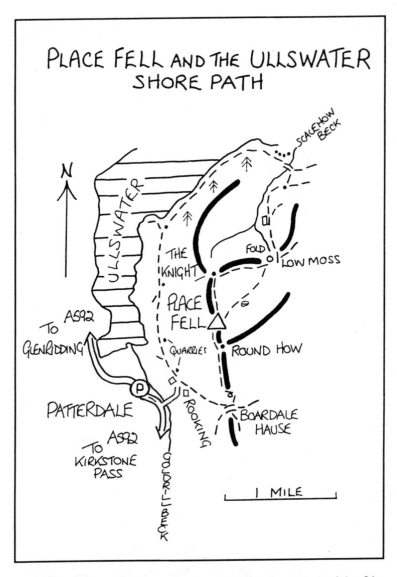

sheepfold, passing a sizeable unnamed tarn. Either way, pass to the right of the sheepfold and when the path forks take the left fork descending the right bank of Low Moss Gill.

We once paused for a 'breather' just below this path fork when to our delight a small herd of deer emerged out of the hanging valley feeding Scalehow Beck. They picked their way daintily across the fellside above Low Moss Gill, barely two hundred yards from our now motionless and barely-breathing forms, before disappearing over the Low Moss saddle.

The path improves as you descend and passes a derelict quarry building. Below this the path forks. Follow the left-hand fork. To your left Scalehow Beck tumbles out of its hanging valley, and reinforced by the waters of Low Moss Gill redoubles the noise and volume of its cascades. Ahead, the view over the lower reaches of Ullswater, backed by the far blue domes of Crossfell and its satellites, widens with every turn of the path. The path closes with the beck near a cascade before veering right to pass between some large boulders. Leave it here and descend steepish grass to join a lower path. Turn left along this to cross a footbridge over Scalehow Beck. Beyond this climb up alongside a wall, swing right round a wall corner and follow the upper path at a fork.

Ullswater lies below now, and prominent across it is Gowbarrow Fell. Along the lakeshore at its foot Wordsworth saw his much acclaimed and sometimes mocked daffodils. The castle-like building is Lyulph's Tower. As the path picks its delightful way around the rocky, wooded, lake-lapped flank of Place Fell the view ahead constantly changes. At first the eye looks deep into Glencoyne, guarded by Greenside (White Stones) and the dark bulk of Sheffield Pike. As you go, Birkhouse Moor (hiding Helvellyn Catstycam), Nethermost Pike and Dollywaggon Pike slowly march into view. Roughly a mile and a half after rounding the wall corner Silver Bay and its pebbly beach is reached. Here the path divides near a large cairn. Climb the left fork up a rocky ravine to a grassy saddle and fine viewpoint.

Distantly ahead is the gap of Kirkstone Pass, dividing Stony Cove Pike, on the left, from Red Screes. To your right, across the head of Ullswater, Grisedale funnels between the dark dome of St. Sunday Crag and the spiny sun-kissed Helvellyn 'edges' towards distant Seat Sandal. Head across the fellside, ignoring all right forks, along a well constructed old quarry path which passes above, below and through evidence of its former use. Beyond a final quarry the path leads down to the footbridge over a beck at the foot of the climb to Boardale Hause to rejoin your outward route.

Walk 10   **8 miles**
            3,000 feet of ascent

Helvellyn via Dunmail Raise

Helvellyn is most easily climbed from the west, from Wythburn Church or The Swirls car park at the foot of Helvellyn Gill. These 'tourist' routes, however, are eroded paths with little to recommend them save their brevity. An ascent from Dunmail Raise, although a little longer, is far more interesting, hardly more arduous and advantageously uses the Wythburn 'tourist' path for a quick and safe descent.

Parking/Start: The lay-by on the eastern verge of the A591 where it crosses Dunmail Raise, just north of the Dunmail Field Centre building. (GR:329113).

The huge sprawling cairn in the centre of the double-carriageway on the crest of the pass reputedly marks the burial place of Dunmail, last King of Cumberland, allegedly slain in battle against the Anglo-Saxons here. History, however, rebukes legend and informs us that Dunmail died peacefully in Rome, with his boots on! I've also read somewhere that in times past travellers over the Raise were forced to run the gauntlet of a gibbet, and possibly its ghastly burden. Incidentally, I've always found this mountain defile a brooding, cheerless place, even on the sunniest day and long before I knew its history. As a young friend of mine is wont to say, 'This place gives me bad vibes, man.'

Walk along the verge to the most northerly stile. Cross it and follow a path climbing gradually leftwards towards the narrow mouth of the valley of Raise Beck. Once in the defile the path, which has been recently renovated, becomes rockier and steeper, clinging to the right bank of the beck. Here, legend whispers that survivors of the slaughter on the Raise fled this way carrying their dead king's crown which they hurled into the depths of Grisedale Tarn out of the clutches of the invaders, and that their ghosts still repeat this loyal task. History, paraphrasing Henry Ford, snarls in our other ear that 'Legend is bunk'. As a graduate historian I should endorse the latter, but I've got to admit that sometimes legends are lots more fun.

The angle eases eventually and the path emerges on to a grassy saddle dividing Seat Sandal and the piquantly named Willie Wife Moor and overlooking Grisedale Tarn. The steep north-western flank of Fairfield dominates the far shore of the tarn. The obvious saddle below and to the left of Fairfield is Deepdale Hause with a narrow ridge climbing beyond it towards the summit of St. Sunday Crag. To your right a path heads across the shaly north-eastern flank of Seat Sandal into the gap of Grisedale Hause. You descend gently from the saddle along a faint path across the northern shore of the tarn to join a path climbing leftwards up the eroded zig-zags whose ascent is the hardest part of the walk. Eventually the angle eases and the path slants

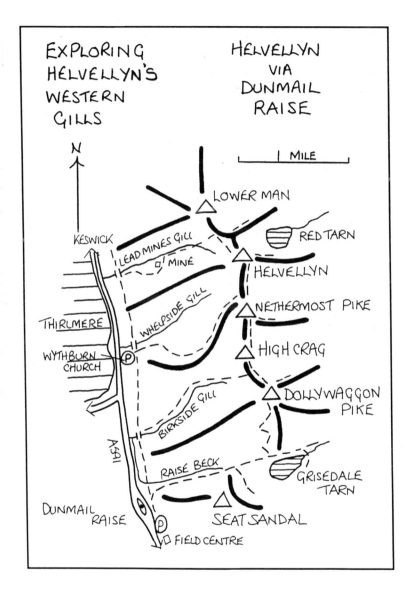

north-westerly on to a ridge whose right flank fall precipitously into the depths of Cock Cove. The 'tourist' path veers away from the fell rim and scuttles around the west flank, missing the summit of Dollywaggon. Don't be tempted by it or you will forfeit all that makes this walk truly enjoyable. Dollywaggon is just the first of a trio of high and handsome fells to be traversed before Helvellyn is 'conquered'. All fellwalkers worth their salt acquire to some degree the voracious appetite of the 'peak-bagger', and they don't count if you scurry around the flanks.

So ignore the path and climb right (an old rusting boundary post is a good point to break away if you haven't already) and follow the fell rim around and above Cock Cove to reach the cairn crowning the grassy dome of Dollywaggon Pike, 2,814 feet. Northwards now piles the eastern scarp whose airy rim will be your pathway to the far dome of Helvellyn. (Now follow the directions given in Walk 5, from "From the Dollywaggon cairn" to "you can't go wrong".)

Walk back from the trig-point, cross over the summit rocks, pass the shelter and descend the worn 'tourist' path into the dip below Nethermost Pike. Should you still be full of vim and vigour you could return over the switchback of Nethermost Pike, High Crag and Dollywaggon Pike and enjoy the views from a different angle. If you feel, however, that you have done enough climbing for today then turn right down the path forking right, above High Crags and the slope falling steeply into the depths of Whelpside Gill, and ultimately down to Wythburn Church. Fairly soon after entering the woods clothing the lower western flanks of Helvellyn you will emerge on to a crossing path near a metal gate and a signpost 'Dunmail Raise/Swirls'. Turn left along this path, eventually to emerge out of the woods on to the bank of creamily cascading Birkside Gill. Cross the footbridge over the gill and follow the path beyond, shortly to cross Raise Beck and reach the stile leading on to Dunmail Raise.

Walk 11 Varies according to which option you take

Exploring Helvellyn's Western Gills

Viewed from the western fells Helvellyn is remarkable only for its height and brawny shoulders. The mountain's western flank is a largely grassy slope of a uniform steepness whose base is clothed in trees. This flank, however, is riven by deep gills which remain largely unexplored, the popular "tourist' paths from Wythburn Church and The Swirls car park taking a treadmill line up the open fellside above the gills. For the more adventurous, the fellwalker-cum-naturalist, or the seeker after solitude, which can amazingly be found on Helvellyn even amid the hubbub of a Bank Holiday, one of the two gills described below should prove interesting.

Parking/Start: The car park behind Wythburn Church. (GR:325136).

BIRKSIDE GILL

Follow the worn path up through the woods to a crossing path near a gate, signposted 'Swirls/Dunmail Raise'. Turn right along this path, following the 'Dunmail Raise' sign, until it emerges out of the woods near a footbridge spanning Birkside Gill. Do not cross the bridge but turn left and climb up alongside a series of splendid cascades. Depending upon the amount of water spilling down, scramble up the rocky bed of the gill, choosing a line to suit your nerves. Above the falls the angle eases slightly, the trees on the left fall away, and a blocked-up mine entrance should be spotted among the scree spilling down the left bank of the gill. Above this, the gill twists and climbs in a succession of cascades and rocky slots which again, according to the amount of falling water and how brave you are feeling that day, give some entertaining scrambling. On a recent early August ascent these rocky steps and their bounding banks were veritable hanging gardens of wild flowers. An enthusiastic but inexpert botanist, I managed to list Common Sundew, Common Milkwort, Bog Asphodel, Yellow Mountain and Starry Saxifrage, Golden Rod, Tormentil, Wild Thyme, Heath Bedstraw, Devils Bit Scabious, Lady's Mantle, Alpine Lady's Mantle, Harebell, Self-Heal, Bilberry, Heather and Bell Heather, Foxglove, Slender St. John's Wort and Herb Robert.

At around two thousand feet above sea level the gill walls begin to fall back, the view behind opens up and the beck eventually sinks into a swamp. Climb up the steepish grass slope above to emerge on to the 'tourist' path crossing the main ridge in the saddle between Dollywaggon Pike and High Crag. Here, the ground falls steeply away below your toe-caps into the depths of Ruthwaite Cove. Beyond, Ullswater's gleaming surface, given the time of year, is be-speckled with multifarious sailing vessels. Hard Tarn, possibly the loveliest of Lakeland's high mountain tarns, lies cupped in its slabby bed at the foot of High Crag's craggy east flank. A commanding presence beyond Ruthwaite Cove is the gully-riven dome of St. Sunday Crag.

Depending upon your fitness and the blessings of the weather, your options now can be varied and energetic. The most obvious route is to head northwards to Helvellyn over High Crag and Nethermost Pike, descending back to Wythburn Church, as per Walk 10. Or you could climb right, on to the summit of Dollywaggon Pike and descend north-easterly down The Tongue for a short way before slanting left down a grassy rake into Ruthwaite Cove and cross it to reach Hard Tarn. You could then wend north in an up and down, in and out, exploration of the splendid eastern coves, climbing back up on to the summit ridge by way of Nethermost Edge, Striding Edge or Swirrel Edge, and descending by the 'tourist' path or even Lead Mines Gill. A tortuous, arduous and pointless route some might say. In this daft and sweaty game, however, these apparently pointless routes often reap the finest rewards — the discovery of the secret corners of a Lakeland fell; the fox, squirrel, deer, bird or flower spotted; the lovely unnamed pool or cascade lunched by; the greening into the fell of old mine or quarry; the startling and unusual view of a thought-familiar fell or valley.

LEAD MINES GILL

Follow the route for Birkside Gill as far as the crossing path in the woods. Turn left along this path, following the 'Swirls' sign. Eventually this forest path passes to the right of a recently felled area, giving a view over Thirlmere and of the fells beyond. A stile in a fence on to the bank of a gill, unnamed on the two-and-a-half-inch map, which I have taken the liberty to christen Lead Mines Gill. You will subsequently discover why, but in fact careful inspection of the ground hereabouts will reveal partially overgrown spoil heaps, clear evidence of past mining. Don't cross the footbridge over the gill, but climb up its right bank to pass above a waterfall. Bear right towards the edge of the woods where a path climbs steeply alongside the forest fence before slanting left across the steep bank of the gill. As you climb look down into the bed of the gill to see the remains of a 'sledgate'. This was a ramp down which 'trams' or ore would be lowered by a winch. In earlier times men would steer ore-laden sleds, or 'trailbarrows', down the fellside, running before them like a horse. The path eventually passes derelict workshops before emerging on to the flat top of a large spoil heap choking the bed of the gill.

Late one summer afternoon, after a hot and energetic day in the sun, I was laid on my back on this spoil heap, head pillowed on my pack and eyes closed. A shadow flitting over my face brought me erect and, startled, I gawped up at what appeared to be a large bird, with a man hanging in its jaws, floating silently across the gill. I realised almost immediately that it was a hang-glider and later that same day was to see it again, grounded and ungainly now, on the shore of Rydal Water. Strange things happen when you doze in the secret corners of the magical Lakeland fells!

Undoubtedly, the upper section of the gill is less interesting. Given the time of year, however, there are numerous wild flowers and I've spotted the reasonably uncommon ring-ouzel drinking from a high pool. The ever expanding view at your back is also a good excuse for a 'breather'. Above the spoil heap a steep and trackless climb up either bank of the gill leads on to a grassy fellside which eases out into the dip between Helvellyn Lower Man and Helvellyn, and a junction with the worn path along the summit ridge. Turn right along this path shortly to reach the trig-point, with the slightly higher summit rocks of Helvellyn, 3,116 feet, rising just beyond.

As with Birkside Gill you now have options open to you. You could descend immediately to Wythburn Church by the 'tourist' path, or you could return to the church by reversing Walk 10, or even descend Birkside Gill. Imaginative scrutiny of the map brings its own unique reward.

THE DODS

Walk 12

**14 miles
3,200 feet of ascent**

Aira Force, Hartside and Great Dod

A walk of interesting contrasts, ranging from the crowded environs of Aira Force to the spacious grassy domes of the Helvellyn Dods, enfolding the lonely upland valley of Deepdale. The path twisting up the flank of the Brown Hills is a delightful prelude to the ascent of Hartside, an apparently seldom-visited two thousand footer. The Dods give easy high-level walking and panoramic views.

Parking/Start: The National Trust car park at the foot of Aira Force. (GR:401201).

Follow the path to Aira Force. After crossing the footbridge over the beck the path on the far side divides. Take the lower left-hand path. Notice the magnificent pine trees to your left. When the walls of the gill close in the sound of cascading water will be heard ahead. Shortly the path divides again. Take the lower left-hand branch down to and across the stone bridge over the beck. Just beyond the bridge look up for a splendid view of Aira Force spanned by a higher bridge. Climb leftwards up steps. At the top of the steps turn down left then shortly right to a gate at the edge of a wood. Follow the path through the wood to emerge into a car park on the verge of the A5091. Cross the road to a stile in the fence. Follow the path beyond, which slants gently right across the fellside above Glencoyne Park. It offers a splendid view of the head of Ullswater and its surrounding fells. Eventually a stile leads over a wall and the path crosses the upper rim of a plantation of splendid trees. Beyond the plantation the path twists steeply upwards before levelling out and passing through a gap in a wall. Across Glencoyne, Sheffield Pike blocks the view ahead.

Beyond the gap a path is joined and followed leftwards to a cairn and path fork. Follow the right fork, cairned, across the fellside sloping left into Glencoyne. After passing over a crossing path it virtually disappears. Look ahead for a broken wall climbing the fellside and head for a gap. Away to your left now, framed in the gap between Sheffield Pike and White Stones, Catstycam's elegant cone superimposes itself on Helvellyn's impersonation of Table Mountain.

Go through the gap in the wall and climb alongside it for a short way until it crosses a slight dip. Leave the wall now and climb leftwards, west-north-west, up a heathery and deceptively steep fellside to emerge on to the broad

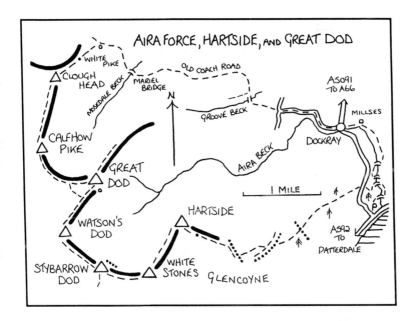

grassy south-east summit of Hartside. Walk north-westerly across a slight dip to reach the cairn crowning the true summit of Hartside, 2,480 feet. The grassy cone of Great Dod, the high point of the walk, rises challengingly ahead and barely a mile away across the lonely swampy depths of Deepdale. Before stepping on to this summit, however, you have to surmount the grassy domes encircling the head of this valley. Just south of Hartside's cairn is a stony trench, which appears to be man-made but to serve what purpose I've no idea. It does make a useful wind shelter should you feel in need of a 'breather'.

From Hartside your way is south-westerly, down onto a broad grassy saddle followed by an easy climb to the cairn crowning White Stones, 2,608 feet. (On some older maps the name emblazoned on this summit is 'Greenside'). From White Stones head west down on to another broad grassy saddle followed by a steepish pull up on to the north-eastern and highest summit of Stybarrow Dod, 2,765 feet. A nearby and apparently purposeless length of wall does, however, come in useful as a wind break. Now you are upon the high grassy watershed of the Helvellyn Dods the views become panoramic. Arrayed in a great arc from Coniston Old Man to Blencathra are the cream of Lakeland's lovely lumpy high fells. From here one clear September afternoon we argued whether or not it was the faint blue hills of Ireland or the Isle of Man we could see through a gap in this skyline. The unfamiliar configuration of these hills, compared to the frequently seen outline of Man, convinced me that it was Ireland. I failed to take note, however, in which gap they were framed so have no bearing to prove it.

From Stybarrow Dod a broad grassy ridge 'zigs' north-westerly to culminate in the summit of Watson's Dod, 2,588 feet. It then 'zags' north-easterly to merge into the grassy summit dome of Great Dod, 2,811 feet. A wind shelter, passed just to the south of the summit cairn, provides a good excuse for a 'breather'. From Great Dod there is a fine view northwards of the deeply cloven multi-ridged Threlkeld flank of Blencathra.

Now descend west, then north-westerly, along the main ridge to 'bag' Calfhow Pike, 2,166 feet, a brash rocky cone set amidst brawny sprawling grass domes. Then a more typical Dods hike just east of north collects the summit of Clough Head, 2,381 feet, where the high grassy promenade of the Dods comes to a precipitous end. There are fine views of Skiddaw, Blencathra and the Vale of Derwentwater.

Now descend north-easterly over White Pike and join the Old Coach Road near a sheepfold. There appears to be little evidence of coaches ever passing this way. It was more likely built to service the local quarries. Turn right and follow this track eventually to emerge on to a junction of tarmac roads at Red Moss. Now follow the road down to Dockray and a junction with the A5091. Cross the A5091 and go through an opening to the right of Dockray Cottage, signposted 'Aira Force/Ulcat Row'. This path passes close to the Aira Beck then between the buildings at Millses before swinging right to a three-fingered signpost. Follow the Aira Force indicator. The left bank of Aira Beck can be followed down to the car park. It's more interesting, however, to cross to the right bank by the footbridge near High Force, recrossing to the left bank by the bridge overlooking Aira Force and so back down to the car park.

Walk 13

11 miles
3,500 feet of ascent

Around St. John's in the Vale via High Rigg and Fisher's Wife's Rake

This round of the fells enfolding the lovely valley of St. John's in the Vale is a little contrived, not a natural 'horseshoe'. Nevertheless, it is none the worse for all that, combining widespread and ever-changing views with some fairly arduous fellwalking. On the rugged western flanks of the Helvellyn Dods mysterious and largely neglected paths, like Fisher's Wife's Rake, wind steeply up between crag and deeply-cloven gill to end by lonely lichened sheepfolds. Don't be deceived by this one — by the time you've finished you'll know you've had a great walk.

Parking/start: Legburthwaite car park and picnic site. (GR:318196). Follow the B5322 where it forks off the A591 Ambleside-Keswick near Stanah. Pass, on your right, the wooden Youth Hostel to reach, also on your right, a pair of semi-detached houses painted half pale green and half white at the time of writing. Look for an opening opposite these houses near some sheds. Turn into this opening, which leads down into the car park and picnic site.

Go through a gate at the rear of the car park on to a road. Turn left and follow this to a gate. Go through the gate and turn right along the verge of the A591, crossing a bridge over St. John's Beck, to a stile on your right. Cross this and, when the path beyond shortly forks, follow the left fork. A steepish climb through some magnificent pines ultimately leads on to the ridge crest. A wall gap in a dip leads to a rocky eminence crowned by a cairn. Pause here for a 'breather' and to take in the High Rigg ridge unfolding ahead, and St. John's in the Vale unrolling its verdant carpet under the shadow of the gill-cloven Dods to the very foot of Blencathra's sharply pleated Threlkeld flank. Look back and glimpse a gleaming segment of tree-thronged Thirlmere.

Continue along the ridge before swinging left to cross a stile in a fence. Descend slightly left around a hillock, then swing right to a fork. Take the left fork along the left side of a hollow. Climb left out of the hollow and down to a stile near a wall corner. Cross this and climb alongside a wall before swinging left then right around a tiny swamp tarn. On a recent May visit I found its surface a delight of flowering Bogbean, described by William Curtis in his 'Flora Londonensis' as 'one of the most beautiful plants this country can boast'. Shortly the wall veers away. Continue on to the beckoning rocks and cairn crowning the lowly summit of High Rigg, 1,163 feet. Lowly or not, the fell is a fine viewpoint. Skiddaw and Blencathra look their best, and north-

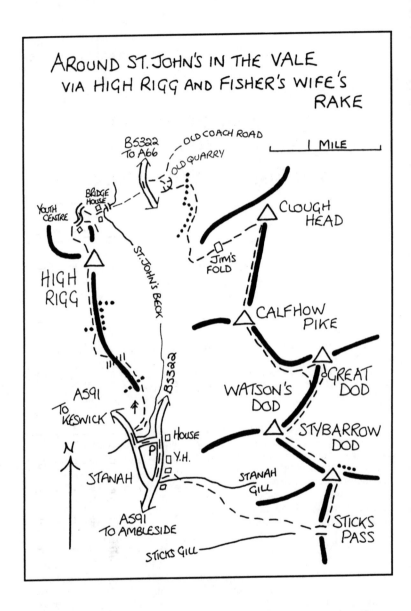

westerly, beyond the white walls of Keswick and gleaming segments of Derwentwater and Bassenthwaite Lake, rise the dark delectable cones and domes of the Coledale and Newlands fells.

Descend beyond the cairn, twisting left then right into a hollow and down to emerge on to a crossing track near a plantation. Turn right along this on to its tarmac continuation, passing the Carlisle Diocese Youth Centre and a chapel. Continue downhill, ignoring a gate/stile signposted 'Public Bridleway/ St. John's in the Vale'. Just beyond, where the road curves left, go right down the bank to a narrow gate in a wall. Descend between becks to cross a clapper bridge near their confluence. Continue down to cross a footbridge over a beck. Go between Bridge House and a barn, then turn left in front of the house and alongside St. John's Beck. Shortly cross this beck by a footbridge and turn left alongside a fence. Cross a stile and continue alongside the fence to a gate. Beyond this turn right up a sunken grassy path alongside a wall before veering left across a field to a stile. Cross the stile and follow the rough track beyond to emerge on to the B5322. Turn left along this, shortly to see a signpost 'Matterdale/unsuitable for motors' directing you into a walled lane to your right. Pass through a gate and climb the stony track beyond twisting up towards the spoil heaps of disused Hill Top Quarries. Look for a stile straddling a fence to your right, where the wall turns away. Cross this, pass a white path marker on a boulder and climb directly up the spoil heaps on to a terrace. Turn right, shortly to see a marker on a stone and a 'footpath' fingerpost pointing left to a path climbing the fellside alongside a fence. Climb this to cross a stile in a fence followed by a stile over a wall.

Turn right and follow a path alongside the wall. When the wall dips into a hollow follow a path forking leftwards. Shortly fork right along a path crossing the fellside above the hollow to reach a wall corner. Continue with a narrow path across the stony fellside between the wall/fence and the base of vegetated Wanthwaite Crags. Beyond the wall/fence's highest point the path climbs towards the base of the crags as it approaches Fisher's Wife's Rake, the shaly chute that is the only breach in these craggy Dod flanks. The path turns around the corner of the crag and climbs steeply, close under the bounding rocks to its left. Eventually it moves away from the rocks to slant right over a badly eroded section. A series of delightful grassy zig-zags follow which pass above the rugged head of Sandbed Gill before leaning back into the grasslands of the Dod high country. Here the path becomes indistinct and, although the two-and-a-half-inch map shows it leading directly to Jim's Fold, I've always had to cast about before finding it. Don't ask me who Fisher or his wife were or why Jim had his well-constructed sheepfold here — I haven't a clue!

From Jim's Fold head north-easterly over tussocky grass to reach the cairn and wind-shelter crowning Clough Head, 2,381 feet. From Clough Head a faint path dips south-south-west down the broad grassy ridge before rising to cross the rocky outcrop of Calfhow Pike, 2,166 feet, unique in this Lakeland corner packed with brawny grassy fells. Beyond Calfhow Pike the path climbs south-east towards Great Dod. About three hundred feet below the top a by-pass path forks right. Ignore this and climb on to reach the cairn crowning Great Dod, 2,811 feet, the high point of the walk.

Walk past a wind shelter and head south-westerly down the grassy ridge to rejoin the 'by-pass' path. When Watson's Dod looms ahead it performs the same shabby trick. Ignore it again and climb gradually west to reach the cairn crowning Watson's Dod, 2,588 feet. The broad grassy summit ridge now 'zigs' south-easterly to a short steepish climb onto the grassy northern and highest top of Stybarrow Dod, 2,765 feet. Head south-west over the lower top then down on to the grassy saddle of Sticks Pass. A smart right turn here takes you across the head of Sticks Gill and down the well-worn path that ultimately brings you to the hamlet of Stanah and the B5322. Turn right along the road to reach the car park.

MARATHON

Shap to Wasdale Head

Walk 14
                                                       30 miles
                                              9,000 feet of ascent

THIS is one for the walker who likes a challenge. It can be done in the daylight hours of a June day by a relatively unfit walker. Honestly, I've done it! I walked it some years ago whilst a member of the Yorkshire Ramblers' Club, who have a fine tradition of 'long walking'. To have their customary support party supplying food, drink and moral support en route undoubtedly had considerable influence on my ultimate success. In contrast to the rest of the walks in this guidebook, which are oftimes repeated old favourites, I have to be honest and say I've never again summoned up the required energy to repeat this marathon. Nevertheless, I remember it with modest pride and hope the description below of our route will encourage a reader, or readers, to 'have a go'. Whether you succeed or go down in gallant defeat you'll never regret or forget your attempt.

The permutations of possible routes linking Shap to Wasdale Head are not endless but certainly varied. I will describe the route we took, which didn't start strictly in Shap but further south at Wasdale Bridge (GR:561083) on the A6. I will add a possible start from Shap, linking with our route on Gatesgarth Pass, which could be considered more proper.

Leaving the A6, we passed through the Shap Pink Granite Quarry and headed up on to the summit of Wasdale Pike. A broad boggy ridge led us south-west then west over Great Yarlside to the handsome cairn crowning Harrop Pike, 2089 feet. A boggy dip west brought us to the cairn and crumbling old survey post, relic of the Haweswater Dam construction, crowning Tarn Crag, 2178 feet. A north-westerly then northerly heading fence led us down to the gate at the head of Mosedale. A slanting climb through the old quarries north of swampy Brownhowe Bottom brought us on to Gatesgarth Pass and a junction with the well-worn path climbing on to Harter Fell, 2552 feet. A descent to Nan Bield was followed by a climb on to Mardale Ill Bell, 2496 feet. Our next objective, the graceful chimney-like cairn of Thornthwaite Crag, 2572 feet, beckoned on the western skyline, so we headed directly to it. On arrival below this splendid edifice we passed through a gap in its supporting wall and, turning right, followed this wall down into the saddle of Threshthwaite Mouth. A surprisingly steep and rocky scramble, in this enclave of largely grassy hills, led us up the far slope and on to the broad grassy summit of Stony Cove Pike, 2503 feet. Beyond the cairn a wall gap led us alongside a westerly, ultimately veering south-westerly, wall which, with a short climb over St. Raven's Edge, led us down to Kirkstone Pass. Here, the Yorkshire Ramblers' support team had set up shop below Red Screes and plied us with very welcome food and drink.

For 'afters', the steep thousand foot scramble up Red Screes was somewhat indigestible. Leaving Red Screes, 2545 feet, we headed west through a gap in a crossing wall to follow a north-westerly heading wall down on to the saddle of Scandale Pass. The old fence stanchions then led us in a north-westerly to south-westerly dog leg around Bakerstones Moss, finishing in a steepish climb to a junction with the eroded 'Fairfield Horseshoe' path running alongside the wall crowning Dove Crag. Turning right, we followed this path past the summit cairn of Dove Crag, 2598 feet. Rockier Hart Crag, 2698 feet, led down to Link Hause, and a further climb north-west, west, then north-west, led to the summit cairn of Fairfield, 2863 feet, the high point of the walk. We then dropped west to Grisedale Hause, and continued down Little Tongue Gill to emerge on to the A591 just above the bad corner at Mill Bridge.

The Yorkshire Ramblers' support team were manning a feeding point just down the minor road opposite. We had been misinformed about this and turned left down the A591 into Grasmere in what was to be a fruitless search for them. In desperation we dived into a pub to quench our thirst, and it took great strength of character to emerge again after one glorious pint and put our throbbing feet back to the quest. Abandoning all hope of further refreshment, we set off up the Easedale Road, luckily to encounter other replete Yorkshire Ramblers emerging on to it from the far end of the minor road mentioned above. Sending our fittest member off for supplies, the rest of us collapsed on the grass verge.

Replete once more, we headed up the well-trodden track past Sour Milk Gill to Easedale Tarn. Passing the tarn, we climbed under the dramatic cone of Belles Knott eventually to emerge on to the watershed about half-a-mile south-east of Sergeant Man. We then traversed across the southern flank of Sergeant Man on to the broad saddle between High Raise and Thunacar Knott. From here a westerly heading took us down to the crest of Stake Pass. We then followed one of Lakeland's boggiest paths south-westerly across the north-west flank of Rossett Pike to emerge on to the shore of Angle Tarn. Suffering by now from an uncontrollable tremor in my hands and knees, or what my cycle racing mates called 'hunger bonk', I collapsed in a quivering heap by the water's edge. Eventually, I thickly plastered a bar of Kendal Mint Cake with honey and forced myself erect. It worked! I was able to make the last climb over Esk Hause and totter down the long descent under the gully-riven crags of Great End and on to the long slant across the shaly slopes of Gable to journey's end. The first drink in the Wastwater Hotel was as the very Elixir of Life.

A possible start from Shap, if you want to do the job properly:

Turn off the main street by the Fire Station and turn left down West Close. Turn almost immediately right and follow the path between houses to emerge into the open fields. Follow the path past the Boggleby Stone and on into the hamlet of Keld. A combination of public footpath, Water Board road, and track lead to a crossing of Thornship Gill above a dam, followed by a boggy climb to a wall guarding Stack House (GR:546124). Climb alongside the wall to a stile near White Crag (GR:538117). Cross this and follow the public bridleway climbing south-westerly out of Wet Sleddale and down into Mosedale. Walk up Mosedale, passing Mosedale Cottage, to a junction with our route as described at the gate at the head of Mosedale.